I NEED TO

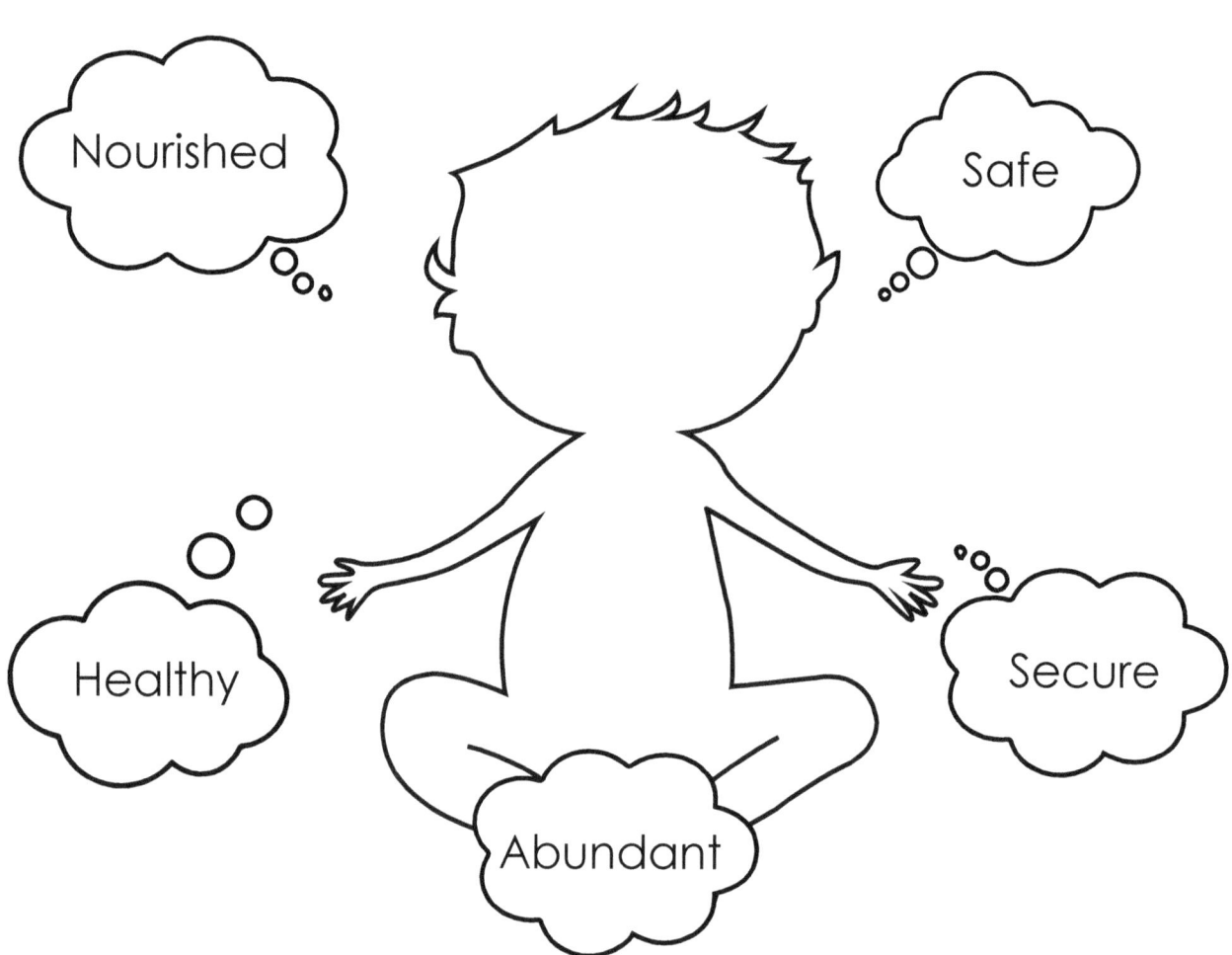

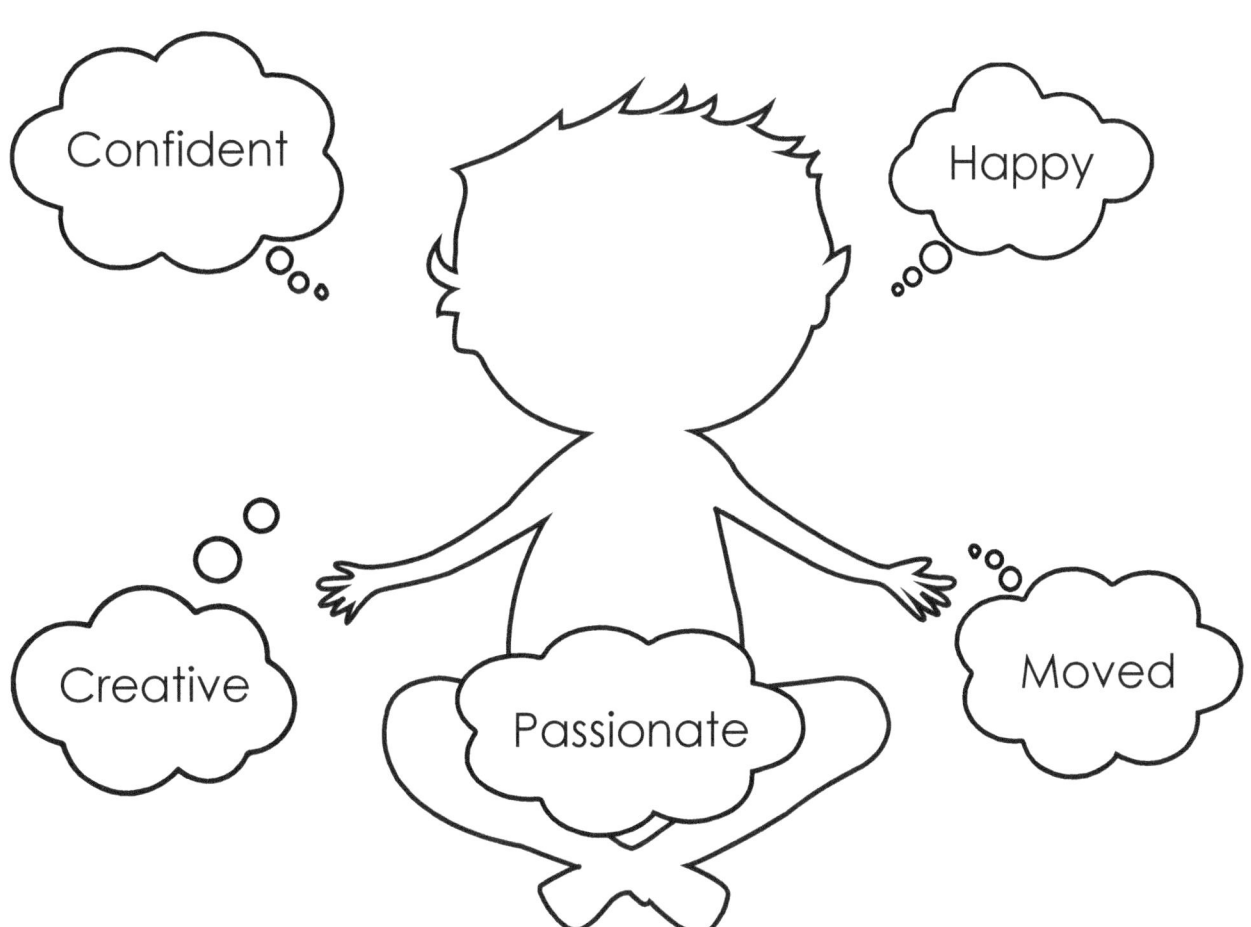

I AM

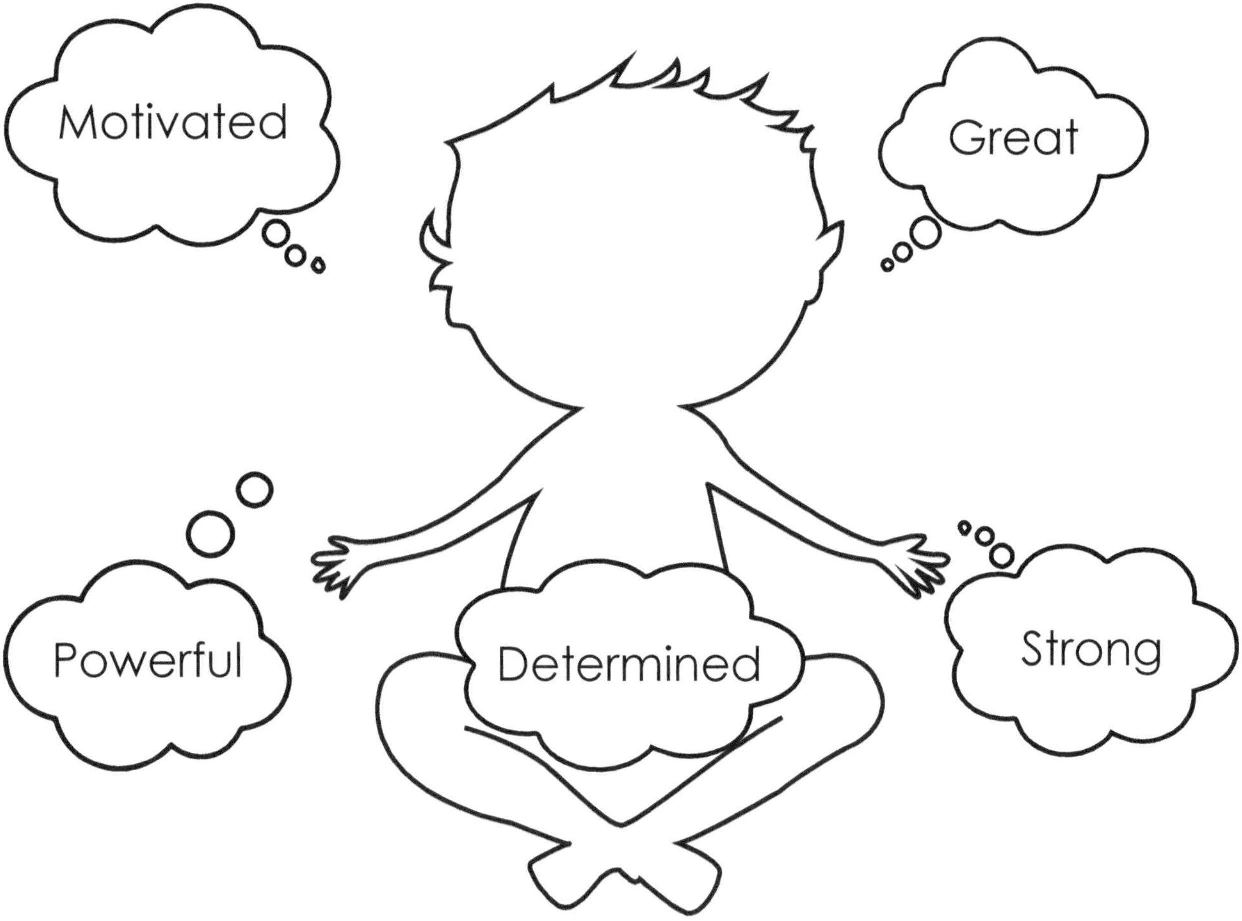

- Motivated
- Great
- Powerful
- Determined
- Strong

I AM

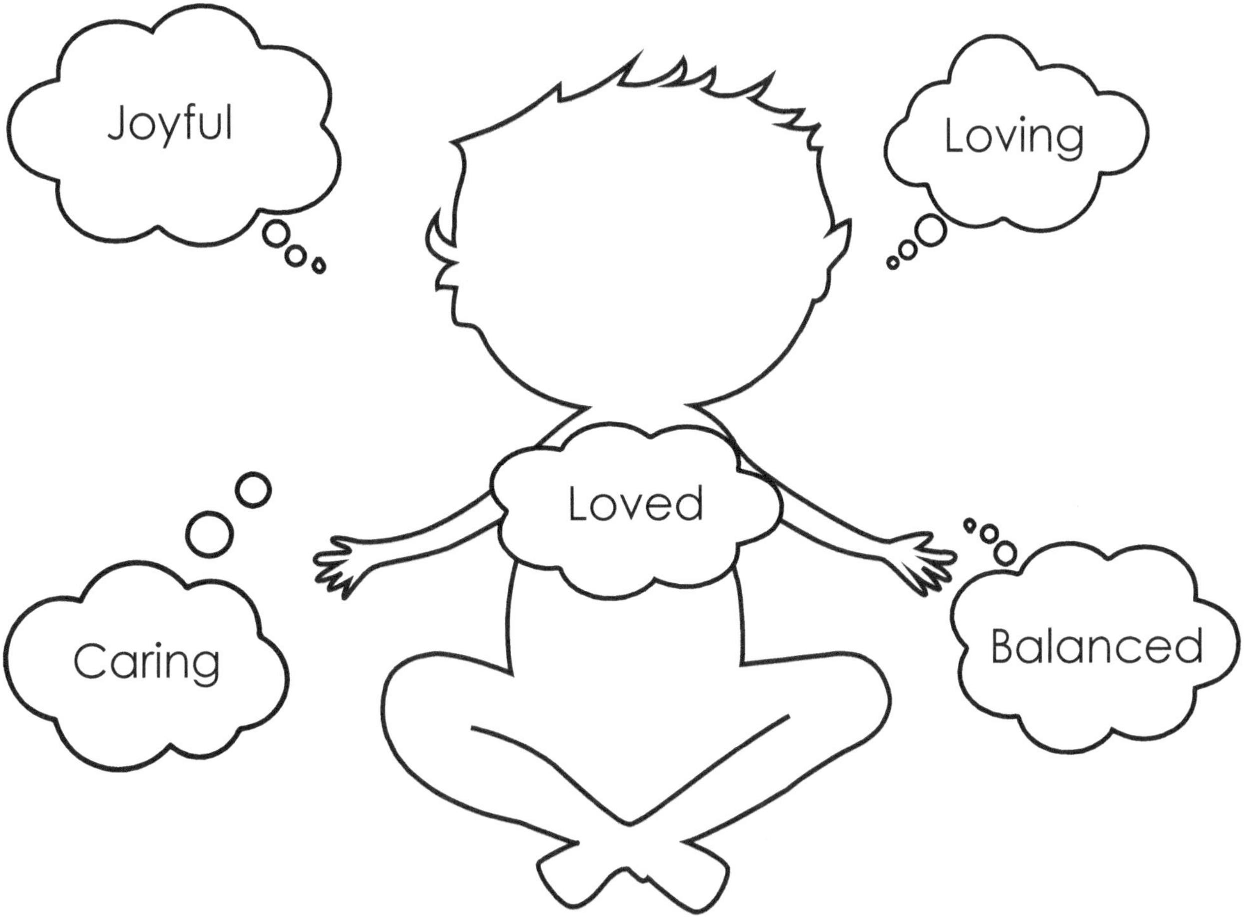

- Joyful
- Loving
- Caring
- Loved
- Balanced

I AM

www.ingramcontent.com/pod-product-compliance
Lightning Source LLC
Chambersburg PA
CBHW061157010526
44118CB00027B/3002